Echoes Through Time

Gitta Bernauer

Order this book online at www.trafford.com
or email orders@trafford.com

Most Trafford titles are also available at major online book retailers.

Print information available on the last page.

ISBN: 978-1-4907-9238-5 (sc)

ISBN: 978-1-4907-9239-2 (hc)

ISBN: 978-1-4907-9237-8 (e)

Library of Congress Control Number: 2018914177

Our mission is to efficiently provide the world's finest, most comprehensive book publishing service, enabling every author to experience
success. To find out how to publish your book, your way, and have it available worldwide, visit us online at www.trafford.com

Trafford rev. 11/30/2018

 www.trafford.com

North America & international
toll-free: 1 888 232 4444 (USA & Canada)
fax: 812 355 4082

Dedicated to:

My mother Erica Bernauer Dec. 10, 1926 - Sept. 14, 2012

My brother Peter Bernauer April 14, 1950 - Sept. 22, 2015

A dear friend Daniel Bedford October 1951 - October 23, 1974

And to Stephen Holland for his encouragement and inspiration
to complete this project.

Candle

Tiny white droplets of wax

Enlaced with gradual intention

Meek and forbearing

In their humble descent

Between times lingering

Lingering, one second, two

The artisan within pondering

Which direction should I take?

Feather

Once enlightened

Now extinguished by the moon

Mantled in darkness, abeyance

A feather now revealed

Draped in white and grey

Gliding from that celestial scene

Phantom of the shadows, now a wandering soul

An ornament unburdened

Only for those who want to see

Bohemian by nature, perpetual transformation

Decreed the Keeper of the Muse

Lifting the facade of hypocrisy

Floating gently downward, audaciously

Below on hallowed ground stands a candle free

With fallow tip quenched out

A relic from the past encouraged now to see

Unravelling life's mystery

Responsive to its need, fading into history

Redeemed to its reality

Now bathed in light, renewed for all to see!

Cherished

In the garden dwelled a single rosebud

So beautiful, unique, so alone

Amidst an array of exotic blooms

Five delicate petals flexible in the wind

Caressing the sun's warmth.

Intimate with the moon's light

Its scent so rare

Prickly thorns displayed

Its survival, natural selection.

Patiently awaiting its admirer

Held in particular esteem

Gently picked and forever cherished

For now it was a rose.

Crusaders on a Quest

From beyond the willows,

Shades of pale-green hue caressing the breeze,

Yonder came the riders,

Crusaders of souls,

They so proclaimed!

Knights to their glory,

Into view they came, gallant, determined,

Determined to play the game.

Perhaps mystical, shrouded,

Fragile intentions eluded

To a realm of imminent doom;

Lives taken needlessly

While whispering the name of the Lord.

These men of the cloth from days of yore,

Knights they be not!

But reapers of the land,

Destroying, fragmenting what we know of man!

Are they history or legend be?

It matters not! In the end, the realization,

This never, ever left,

And the thought remains, as truth be taught,

Where did they go astray?

Beyond the Mist

Beyond the mist,

Where shadows dwell,

Images of light persist.

Darkness surrenders

To the winding road,

Leading to a forest dense.

Glowing embers alive,

Insight into one's soul,

Whispering sounds of peace,

Understanding of self,

A realm hidden from the past.

Reaching beyond boundaries set,

The past's reality awakens

With heaven's warmth,

Now extended within,

Experiencing infinite energy.

Our spirits have now met,

Embraced in one another's bliss.

Echoes

Warm grains of sand underfoot

Infinite in their display

Bathed in moonlight

Glistening beneath the stars

Enveloped by melodic echoes

Of the Spanish guitar

A gift of passion shared

Tomados de la caminamos

Ocasional a lo largo de la playa

Each wave, a greeting

From the spirit of the sea

Cherished by humanity

Courage, an ardent quest

Beyond the gloaming

We will be beloved

For all eternity.

The Keeper

In the distance, off the rocky shore

Stood an ancient Celtic lighthouse

Resting upon the island alone,

Accompanied by its keeper.

The beacon of hope,

Be it in the sea of tranquility

Or conquering storms,

His courage is the guiding light.

Serenity calms his spirit

For yet another fortnight.

Within this milieu,

Beneath the canopy of twinkling stars,

While the moonlit sea gleams,

The infinite galaxy of Milky Way,

Where seabirds freely soar languidly

Into the midnight sky,

His soul's reflection

With endless depth

Captured my heart; serendipity!

Love or Romance

She stroked his aging face,

Fingertips guided by gentle lines

Deep from life's long path.

Untold stories now unfold,

No special sequence, no time.

Romance, one's great love,

One's great defeat, to meet;

Torn between the two

When, in the ending of it all,

The deepest infinite line

Portraying love

Was the result of man's greatest grief!

An Autumn Eve

Relaxing in the evening shade,

Enjoying memories of days now past,

Feeling the cool, fresh autumn breeze,

Among the ancient willow trees.

Walking gradually toward the stream,

Reflections of the moon are seen.

Gazing upwards, so far away,

Northern lights danced with the Milky Way.

Fallen branches with withered leaves

Drifted casually in search of harmony.

Gracefully perched upon a limb,

A lonesome blue heron slept peacefully.

Enveloped gently by the hands of time,

This passive soul now sauntered by.

Having found the well-worn path,

She perpended over life's repose,

Her arms extended in earnest quest,

Embracing eternity,

The final rest.

Unveiled

On the edge of the dream,

Lingered an aura of serenity,

Woven from fragments of reality,

Though driven unconsciously,

A resurgence of familiarity,

Pointing to aspects of underlying frailty.

The Achilles' heel sees daybreak,

From the realm of the shadow,

Never to be eluded,

Cast aside by vulnerability,

Enhancing love and light,

Expanding consciousness,

Departing from masked illusions,

Healing the child within,

Embracing love divine.

Illumination

A golden hue embraced your tender face,

In gentle illumination,

The passage to our souls,

Guided by a higher entity.

Within the depths of mutual perception,

A spiritual awakening ensued,

Warmth and acceptance led the way,

Surpassing the human endeavour.

Your eyes are the lighthouse to my soul,

Therein dwells enduring love,

A constant reflection of you,

Melding together is a journey,

Of mutual bliss!

Eagle

From above, serenity was seen

Floating in silence,

Spreading both wings,

Gliding into view,

Above the deep green,

Reaching mightily,

Exchanging shadows with,

The monarch of the sky,

For a mere moment

On that particular eve.

Truth

Look around and what you see

Are chaotic souls afire

Sense of truth in this reality

Draped in coats of greed and power

Now members of the Club, "Miscreant".

All senses left behind

Internally distraught

If they'd stop and really look

And search for the light

The affirmation of the truth

The opposite of greed is love

As our teacher reveals

His power is steadfast and true

They cried out for help

He answered their call

"Embrace me," he urged

"For I am your lifelong friend."

Journey Home

Wandering through the mind's inner eye

Searching for thoughts lost

Encountering fragments of momentary reflect

On happiness.

Bliss, harmony, tender heart

Inner strength, an ardent friend

Grasping past glimpses of solitude

While on the path endured.

Footsteps treading cautiously

As the moon's smile glances

In the direction opposite

Enabling the state of sleep.

Dreams escape to reality

Meeting past, present, and future

Crossing the threshold with ease

As heart, mind, and soul

Embrace peace.

Friendship

Friendship, the golden key

Held by those of antiquity

Compassion, the treasured pathway

Open our hearts amid the misery

As the mirror reflects humanity.

Let universal bondage be the way

Felt by all as witnesses

To this widespread tragedy

Hope comes forth from within.

May each tear we shed

Remind us of our frailty

Let us all be selfless

In our own unique way.

Prayers given up for all the perished

And those astray

To be reunited with family, friends

To the open arms

Of our true humanity.

Solitary

The heart and soul of every man

Is mirrored by the light

Interfacing his reality

Of yet a different kind.

His gentle hands extending

To reach that ending point

Whispers are relinquished

Through tears shed years ago.

Alone and often worried

He walks the face of earth

Watching for the signals

Of those who walked before.

Gentle images awakening

The depths of his very soul

His inner spirit remembers

That long walk to the end

To the end of that very road.

Reflecting on life's experiences

Imprinted on that man,

He has conquered solace,

From within his very soul.

Shooting Star

Down the trail steadily,

With a carefree spirit,

Going with the flow.

Meandering through the valley trails,

Beneath a canopy of joy,

Breathing in the air of awakening.

No longer a restless soul,

You come upon a meadow green,

The sun illuminating your journey there.

Pausing for reflection,

You gently place your cycle, blue,

Against the nearby ash wood tree.

Your shoulder finds comfort there,

When an overwhelming inner urge,

Sees you gazing toward the heavens,

As a shooting star passes overhead,

It all makes sense!

Soul Mates

From deep within came a sigh,

Euphoric in nature,

Blissful in rhyme,

Intense beyond the realm of words,

As the two souls intertwined.

Floating beyond the natural world,

Known as heaven in their minds' eye,

Cherishing the moment in this eternity,

There they dwelled in harmony,

Soul mates evermore.

Awakening

Within my heart

Shadows assembled collectively

With acquiescent sighs, reveille

To the depths of my soul

Having dwelled in disarray

Now filled with bliss

As your tender-hearted spirit

Found mine reflective.

The Runner

In the early hours of each day,

His shadow passes by my way;

His stride is constant, paced,

Breathing rhythmically, self-control.

Daily, alone, solitude,

At the mercy of nature's temperament,

Oftentimes I question why.

So elusive yet defined,

The runner in me sighs;

Fatigue has led the way.

For brief moments in our lives,

Your shadow passes by

With a glance

And a shared acknowledgement;

What truly is your quest?

Sentience

One's inner voice, solemn

Arising from spiritual depths

Enlightened, searching

Glimpses of past encounters

Life's acknowledgements

Embracing, experiencing unison

Understanding, pondering

Perpetual interaction

Blissful, whimsical

Familiar entities drifting

Into the warmth within

Encompassing truths

Once withdrawn, now touching

Heart's regality

Unspoken desires fulfilled

Extending beyond daily trivialities

Assured of one's destined reality

Intermittent stepping stones

Heart, mind, soul

Fervent in their quest

To put the past to rest

Ascending to simplicity

Tears, fears forgotten

Having found his way

No longer complacent

Reaching past the shadows

Beginning definitive bonding

Permitting time to slip graciously by

Emphasizing the eternal sigh

Acceptance is the way

The key to love's sanctuary.

Neptune

Beneath the ocean's surface

Where Neptune rules the sea

Could be heard the alluring echoes

From the sirens of the deep,

Heard clearly

As the tide water hits the shore

Passing by Davy Jones's locker

Into the nether world below

Enchanting, timeless

Thereupon the greeting

From the mermaid of your dreams

United now forever

In the deep blue sea.

The Old Cross Keys Inn

Along the road from Belfast to Derry

There rests the Old Cross Keys Inn,

Having endured three hundred years of history,

With the inviting gesture of a thatched roof,

The worn pathway

Displayed brown cobblestones,

Gracefully leads to a latched door.

Permeated within its uneven walls

And fatigued stone floors,

Enchanting and warm,

As the fireplace sits centre stage,

Its hearth a welcome sight,

Unseen spirits of days gone by

Are a comforting thought.

A dark shadow lingered at the doorway.

An invitation was uttered from within

As the gentle wind rustled through the trees:

"Do come in" and "Choose a seat."

The gallery hosted a gathering;

Despite that, he found a place,

Front row center.

He indeed was pleased!

Magic

With eyes so bright and true,

I came upon this Irish lad

Leaning comfortably against

An old gas lamppost;

His shadow intertwined

With the light above,

Streaming magically

Upon the path below.

Mirrored sanity in his eyes

Showed a loving soul,

Divine and altruistic.

His smile reflected

Endless awareness,

Subtle yet subdued.

His hand reached out

For mine in love.

Printed in the United States
By Bookmasters